PRESERVED STEAM ALBUM

David C. Rodgers

Copyright © Jane's Publishing Company Limited 1986

First published in the United Kingdom in 1986 by
Jane's Publishing Company Limited
238 City Road, London EC1V 2PU

ISBN 0 7106 0378 9

Printed by Netherwood Dalton & Co Ltd, Huddersfield

JANE'S

Cover illustrations

Front: Shortly after the early morning mist has cleared Ivatt Class 2
2-6-0 No 46443 bursts out of the 480-yard Foley Park tunnel into the
low winter sunshine and accelerates down the 1 in 100 grade towards
Bewdley hauling a Kidderminster-Arley 'Santa Special' formed of
BR Mk 1 stock in carmine and cream livery. 15 December 1984.
(David C Rodgers)
Pentax MX   50mm Takumar   Kodachrome 25   1/250, f2.6

Back: After leaving Port Soderick, Port Erin-bound trains face a
climb up through Crogga woods before dropping down to Santon,
5¾ miles from Douglas. On its regular working returning to its
home base of Port Erin, Isle of Man Railway dark red-liveried Beyer
Peacock 2-4-0T No 4 *Loch* emerges from the woods with the 1610
from Douglas. 31 May 1983. *(David C Rodgers)*
Pentax MX   135mm Takumar   Kodachrome 25   1/250, f3.5

Right: Probably the most noteworthy British outside cylinder
0-8-0 engines were those of the North Eastern Railway, the first of
which, the Class T, appeared in 1901. A further development was the
T2 (LNER Class Q6) of which 120 superheated engines were built
between 1913 and 1921 to the design of Vincent Raven for heavy
mineral traffic. Withdrawn from Sunderland (South Dock) shed in
1967, No 63395 has been vacuum-fitted and restored to earlier livery
as NER No 2238. She is seen here at Beckhole on the North
Yorkshire Moors Railway with a Pickering train on what was, prior
to closure, a double-track formation. 11 April 1977. *(E P Bobrowski)*
Minolta SRT 101   50mm lens   Kodachrome II   1/250, f3.5

Introduction

Thirty-five years have now elapsed since a small group of enthusiasts took over the operation of the moribund 2 ft 3 in gauge Talyllyn Railway in Wales; from this beginning the railway preservation movement has prospered to become an integral part of the leisure industry. While some lines are operated by private companies or, in the case of the Vale of Rheidol Railway, by British Rail, the majority rely heavily on volunteer labour — men and women from all walks of life united in bringing enjoyment to the growing throng of holidaymakers, tourists or lovers of nostalgia.

In this volume I have tried to cover most of the major private railways from 15 in gauge upwards but sadly space has precluded the inclusion of steam centres, museums and very short lines. Choosing the photographs has been extremely difficult, even frustrating, as I have had to exclude many excellent pictures in order to give a reasonably balanced coverage; if this has led to the omission of any loco or line for which you have a particular affinity, I can only apologise!

In conclusion I would like to express my gratitude to the many photographers who have freely allowed me to use their material, so enabling me to depict a far broader coverage than would otherwise have been possible. My special thanks are due to my wife, Julie, for correcting and typing the manuscript, our two boys, Jonathan and Michael, for assisting with the unenviable task of sorting the slides and expressing their views on picture selection, and finally to Ken Harris of Jane's, Tom Heavyside and Anthony Lambert for their help, advice and constructive criticism.

DAVID C RODGERS
Huddersfield
May 1986

Left: Hopefully scenes such as this will become commonplace when trains once again head north from Horsted Keynes to East Grinstead – the long-term objective of the Bluebell Railway. Former US Army Transportation Corps 0-6-0T, sold to the Southern Railway for use in Southampton docks and latterly BR No 30064, does a spot of shunting at this 5-platform station. Restored to Southern Railway style and decor, this station was the terminus of the electrically worked branch from Haywards Heath which isolated the Bluebell Railway from BR on closure in 1963. 9 April 1977. *(David C Rodgers)*
Pentax SP500   55mm Takumar
Kodachrome II   1/125, f4.5

Above: The gorse is in bloom as, working back to her base at Port Erin, Beyer Peacock 2-4-0T No 4 *Loch* threads Oakhill cutting and approaches the summit of the 2-mile climb at 1 in 65/70 with the 1610 *ex*-Douglas. Beyer Peacock supplied 15 2-4-0Ts for use in the Isle of Man between 1873 and 1926, each batch being slightly larger than the last. No 4 *Loch,* built in 1874, is the oldest of the five surviving active locos, and immediately behind her is third class bogie coach F18 restored to purple lake livery. 31 May 1983. *(David C Rodgers)*
Pentax K1000   50mm Takumar
Kodachrome 25   1/250, f3.8

"The train standing at platform 2 is for Cleobury Mortimer, Tenbury Wells and Woofferton . . . " This timeless scene at Bewdley recreates much of the old charm of rail travel, a true period piece complete with gas lamp. GWR 0-6-0PT No 5764 shunts empty stock opposite Bewdley North signal box. Re-opened in stages from Bridgnorth, the SVR arrived at Bewdley in 1974 and was subsequently extended to Kidderminster ten years later. 16 April 1976. (David C Rodgers) Pentax SP500 55mm Takumar Kodachrome II 1/60, f4.5

The event of 1985 was undoubtedly the return to service of GWR 4-4-0 No 3440 *City of Truro!* Built in 1903, it achieved fame by becoming the first locomotive to exceed 100mph, a speed which was subsequently disputed. Later renumbered No 3717 it was withdrawn in 1931 and presented to York Museum, where it rested until 1957, when it was brought out of retirement for a brief 4-year period before being taken into Swindon Museum. It re-emerged from here in 1984 to be prepared for the celebrations to mark the 150th anniversary of the GWR. Originally unsuperheated, without top feed and having a plain cast chimney, No 3440 has nevertheless been restored to the elaborate Edwardian livery and is a magnificent sight accelerating six GWR coaches away from the Sterns slack with the 1425 Bridgnorth-Kidderminster. 13 October 1985. *(David C Rodgers)*
Pentax K1000 50mm Takumar
Kodachrome 25 1/250, f3.5

Left: Ffestiniog Railway 2-4-0STT *Blanche* approaches the summit of the line some 650 ft above sea level at Llyn Ystradau, one-time temporary terminus on the deviation route between Dduallt and Tanygrisiau. Behind the train is Tanygrisiau Reservoir serving the CEGB Ffestiniog hydro-electric power station; during 'off-peak' periods the water is pumped back to Stwylan Dam over 1000 feet above, allowing the water level to drop by some 18 feet thus revealing the old FR route. *Blanche* and her sister, *Linda*, were built as 0-4-0STs by the Hunslet Engine Co for the Penrhyn Quarry Railway; subsequently both were rebuilt with a leading truck and fitted with tenders, although *Blanche* differs in that she is fitted with a tender cab. 30 May 1985. (David C Rodgers)
Pentax MX   85mm Takumar
Kodachrome 25   1/250, f3.2

Above: A great embankment constructed by William Alexander Madocks between Porthmadog and Boston Lodge permitted a large land reclamation scheme on the estuary of the Afon Glaslyn. Completed in 1811 and known as 'The Cob', it serves two modes of transport – a toll road and the 1 ft 11½ in gauge Ffestiniog Railway. On the latter, 1879-built Fairlie 0-4-4-0T *Merddin Emrys* heads an afternoon train from Porthmadog to Tanygrisiau, then terminus of the line, which was extended one year later for a further 1½ miles to Blaenau Ffestiniog. April 1981. (David C Rodgers)
Pentax K1000   55mm Takumar
Kodachrome 25   1/250, f4

Opposite: Although essentially an LNER design, Class K1 2-6-0 No 62005 did not appear until shortly after nationalisation and, for several years following restoration was painted in LNER apple green livery. However, for a brief period before a major overhaul it was repainted in lined BR black livery and is shown here looking resplendent tackling the 1 in 49 grade at Green End on the North Yorkshire Moors Railway with the 1055 Grosmont-Pickering, the train including three ex-BR Metro-Cammell Pullman cars. 29 April 1984. *(David C Rodgers)*
Pentax MX
50mm Takumar
Kodachrome 25
1/250, f3.5

Left: On the same day No 62005 heads the 1455 Grosmont-Pickering across Goathland Moor, between Moorgates and Ellerbeck summit. Closed in 1965 in favour of the Esk Valley line, the North Yorkshire Moors Railway reopened in 1973, the ceremony being performed by HRH The Duchess of Kent. 29 April 1984. *(David C Rodgers)*
Pentax MX
85mm Takumar
Kodachrome 25
1/250, f3.8

Left: The first 'Atlantic' or 4-4-2 tender engine to be built in Britain was GNR No 990 *Henry Oakley.* Designed by H A Ivatt and built at Doncaster in 1898, it represented a considerable advance in power, and experience gained led to the building from 1902 of perhaps the most celebrated of the type, the GNR 'Large Atlantics'. Until the advent of Gresley's Pacifics No 990 was the only named engine on the GNR. It was withdrawn in 1937 and preserved in York Museum but was restored in 1975 to appear in the Stockton and Darlington 150th anniversary celebrations at Shildon. It later worked for a short season on the KWVR where it is seen leaving Oakworth, its 6 ft 8 in diameter driving wheels hardly suited to the steeply graded branch. June 1977. *(David C Rodgers)*
Pentax SP500   55mm Takumar
Kodachrome 11   1/250, f3.5

Lower left: The end of the line for recently-repainted LMS Class 8F 2-8-0 No 48431 as she stands on arrival lit by gaslight in Oxenhope station, on the Keighley and Worth Valley Railway. Night photography can often produce quite dramatic effects; however a great deal of patience is needed, particularly on preserved lines where passengers tend to congregate around the engine and produce a surreal effect with ghostly images! The 81A (Old Oak Common) shedplate is accurate for the loco was actually built at Swindon and spent a great deal of its life on the GWR and later Western Region, being withdrawn from Bath (Green Park) depot in 1964. Worth Valley staff are only too keen to remind visitors that the GWR finally built a modern heavy freight loco, albeit of LMS design! 16 March 1986. *(David C Rodgers)*
Pentax MX   50mm Takumar
Kodachrome 25   40 secs at f2.8 with fill-in flash

Right: The Worth Valley echoes to the combined exhausts of Fowler Class 4F 0-6-0 No 43924 and 8F 2-8-0 No 8431 as they blast out of Damems loop with a 'Santa Special'. The 4F is shown wearing a diagonal warning stripe prohibiting its use under the 25kV wires south of Crewe and is paired with a tender from Crab No 42765, of similar design to its own but fitted with coal rails. The 8F design was chosen by the Ministry of Supply to be built in other railways' workshops to overcome a critical shortage of freight power during World War II. *(David C Rodgers)*
Pentax MX   85mm Takumar
Kodachrome 25   1/250, f2.8

Left: The Kent and East Sussex Railway, linking Robertsbridge with Headcorn, was probably the most famous of Britain's standard gauge light railways. Pioneered by Colonel Holman F Stephens, the line escaped grouping in 1923 but on nationalisation became part of the Southern Region. Passenger services were restored in 1974, 20 years after withdrawal by BR. The heterogeneous collection of motive power and rolling stock exemplified by this view of No 12 *Marcia*, a tiny Peckett 0-4-0T, climbing Bodiam bank with District Railway first class 4-wheel coach No 100 would surely have delighted its former owner. 25 May 1981.
(Geoff Silcock)
Bronica S2   75mm Nikkor
Ektachrome 64   1/250, f8

Right: The end of the line for *Joem?* For a brief period the Derwent Valley Railway operated a steam service from York (Layerthorpe) using Class J72 0-6-0T No 69023. Although the class dates from 1898 the final 28, including this loco, were not built until BR days in 1950/1! Withdrawn from departmental use in 1966, it re-entered service on the KWVR before moving to the NYMR where it was being restored in 1986 to NER green livery with BR and NER crests, as applied to selected station pilots at York and Newcastle in the late 1950s. At one time the DVR ran through to Cliff Common on the Selby-Market Weighton line, BR at York providing a J27 as normal power. 29 August 1979.
(David C Rodgers)
Pentax SP500
55mm Takumar
Kodachrome 25
1/125, f4.5

Colliery winding gear overshadows Bagnall 0-4-0ST 2450/1931 *J. T. Daly* heading a train for Blythe Bridge away from Dilhorne Colliery on a section of track no longer in use at the start of the 4-mile Foxfield Light Railway in the Potteries. The line has since been reduced by half a mile and now starts at Dilhorne Park, while *J. T. Daly* has been transferred to the Alderney Railway in the Channel Islands. The loco is seen hauling a former LMS bogie scenery van converted to an observation coach, and is banked in the rear by RSH 0-6-0ST 6947/1938. September 1972. *(M Squire)*
Pentax SV   55mm Takumar
Kodachrome 11   1/250, f4

Shafts of sunlight intermingle with sulphurous smoke and steam, so reminiscent of the everyday scene at many larger industrial loco depots 20 years ago, at the Marley Hill depot of the Tanfield Railway. Situated some five miles south-west of Newcastle, the railway is being built on a 3-mile section of the former Tanfield wagonway. Creating the illusion is RSH 0-4-0ST 7409/1948 *Sir Cecil A. Cochrane*. 21 April 1979.
(M Squire)
Pentax SP500   55mm Takumar
Kodachrome 11   1/60, f2

15

Left: For a short period immediately prior to being withdrawn for her 10-year boiler examination, *Blackmore Vale* was repainted in BR Brunswick green lined in orange and black, the livery it carried from April 1950 until withdrawal at the end of SR steam in July 1967, when it was purchased by the Bulleid Preservation Society for £1900. No 34023 is seen soon after leaving Sheffield Park with a train for Horsted Keynes on the Bluebell Railway. 14 October 1984. *(M E Ranieri)*
Nikkormat FTN 50 mm Nikkor
Kodachrome 25 1/250, f2.8

Above: Few readers will fail to be impressed by Bulleid's innovative design of lightweight Pacifics. A total of 110 'West Country' and almost identical 'Battle of Britain' locos with their distinctive 'air-smoothed' casing were introduced at the end of World War II, and with their light (18¾-ton) axle load were capable of being used over most secondary routes on the Southern. 21C123 *Blackmore Vale* is having her high-sided 4500-gallon tender replenished at Sheffield Park, the Dorset coat of arms glinting in the low evening light and contrasting with her malachite green livery. July 1976. *(E P Bobrowski)*
Minolta SRT100 50mm lens
Kodachrome 11 1/250, f2.8

Below: A late afternoon train from Loughborough to Rothley on the Great Central Railway hauled by LNER Class N2 0-6-2T No 4744 is silhouetted crossing Swithland Viaduct, spanning Swithland Reservoir, which supplies much of the water for the city of Leicester. Built for the GNR in 1921 as No 1744, this machine subsequently became BR No 69523 and is the last survivor of a class of 107 locos largely used on Kings Cross suburban services. On withdrawal it was preserved by the Gresley Society and was formerly based on the KWVR. 15 February 1981.
(D Gouldthorpe)
Pentax S1a   35-80 zoom   Agfa CT18
1/250, f5.6

Right: On a day when the thermometer barely registered above freezing, Churchward 2-8-0T No 5224 takes the lightly loaded 1300 Loughborough-Rothley across Swithland viaduct on the Great Central Railway. No 5224 re-entered traffic after a 7-year overhaul in March 1985 and resplendent in early BR black livery, she looks none the worse for her long sojourn in Barry scrapyard. Although far from South Wales, where the 205 engines of this type were principally used on heavy mineral traffic, GW engines were a common sight in Leicester and on occasions were seen on this section to Nottingham. 29 December 1985.
(David C Rodgers)
Pentax K1000   50mm Takumar
Kodachrome 25   1/250, f2.6

A pair of gleaming GWR 14xx 0-4-2Ts with highly polished brass safety valve bonnets simmer outside Buckfastleigh shed on the Dart Valley Railway. The 75-strong class was a familiar sight on light branch passenger and push-pull duties and with 5 ft 2 in diameter driving wheels had a fair turn of speed. Both are now named, No 1420 *Bulliver* and No 1450

Ashburton. 29 August 1977. (M Squire)
Pentax SP500   55mm Takumar
Kodachrome 25   1/125, f5.6

GWR 45xx 2-6-2T No 4555 gently steams through the glorious South Devon countryside as it enters Buckfastleigh on the Dart Valley Railway. Originally a broad gauge branch worked by the South Devon Railway and later absorbed by the GWR, the 9½-mile Totnes-Ashburton line closed in 1962. It reopened seven years later but unfortunately the section beyond Buckfastleigh was severed by the A38 trunk road; however, on the credit side, services now operate into Totnes BR station. The 175-strong 45xx small Prairie tanks were used extensively in the West Country, the first 75 differing from later examples in having only 1000-gallon capacity side tanks, unlike No 4588 on the neighbouring Torbay & Dartmouth Railway. 14 September 1972. *(Andrew Bell)*

Pentax S1a 55mm Takumar
Kodachrome II 1/250, f4

Left: Recreating a nostalgic scene for lovers of East Anglian byeways is LNER Class J15 0-6-0 No 7564 as it prepares to set back into Sheringham station. The North Norfolk Railway's headquarters is at the old M&GN station in Sheringham, while BR's service to Cromer and Norwich runs from a newly-built halt. No fewer than 290 of these diminutive locos were constructed for the GER over a 30-year period and were used throughout former GER territory until the early 1960s, although more than 40 served overseas during World War I. Many received bell-mouthed chimneys, but No 7564 retains its original stove-pipe. 27 August 1984. *(Andrew Bell)*
Mamiya 645   150mm Sekor
Ektachrome Professional 64   1/250, f4

Below: In 1959 the greater part of the Midland and Great Northern Joint Railway, linking the Midlands with the Norfolk coast and penetrating deep into GER territory, closed down. This act was the seed that led to the North Norfolk Railway re-opening the section of line initially from Sheringham to Weybourne and later to Kelling Camp. Having been propelled from Sheringham and posed against the golf course in an area designated as being of outstanding natural beauty, is LNER Class B12/3 No 61572, the only preserved inside cylinder 4-6-0 in Britain. Built by Beyer Peacock in 1928 to Holden's GER design, it was later rebuilt with round-top boiler; it was hoped to have her once again in steam in 1987. 1 October 1977. *(J S Everitt)*
Mamiyaflex C2   Agfachrome 50S
1/250, f5.6

After observing the severe slack over Victoria Bridge, whose cast iron ribs span 200 feet across the River Severn, 'Hall' class 4-6-0 No 4930 *Hagley Hall* storms up the grade towards Arley with a 'Santa Special' from Kidderminster formed of eight ex-BR Mk 1 coaches. Built at Swindon in 1929, it was on restoration paired with a Hawksworth straight-sided tender until an exchange was effected with sister No 6960 shortly before this scene. Restored to main line condition, No 4930 achieved fame when summoned at short notice to Plymouth to deputise for the failed *King George V* on a GW150 railtour during Easter 1985. 9 December 1984. *(David C Rodgers)*
Pentax K1000   85mm Takumar
Kodachrome 25   1/250, f2.5

24

A firm favourite with the author is Ivatt Class 4 2-6-0 No 43106, for she achieved a speed of 82 mph on a railtour organised by the author in February 1967, the only bright spot in a day dominated by a poor performance by a 'Jubilee'. At that time she was based at Carlisle (Kingmoor) but had migrated to Lostock Hall depot near Preston before being withdrawn only days before the end of steam on BR to take refuge on the fledgling SVR as the only survivor of a class of 162. Subsequently she has been restored to main line condition but is seen here at Bewdley, her fireman engaged in the age-old ritual of shovelling out the char from the smokebox. 24 April 1982.
(David C Rodgers)
Pentax K1000   135mm Takumar
Kodachrome 25   1/125, f3.2

25

Above: The Romney, Hythe and Dymchurch Railway was built by the late Captain J E P Howey to serve a section of the Kent coast poorly provided with public transport. Today the railway uses 11 steam locomotives of 6 different types built to approximately one third full size, but operating on 15 in gauge track – roughly one quarter scale. The first batch of engines was built by Davey Paxman & Co in 1925/6 to Henry Greenly's design and they bear a close resemblance to Gresley's LNER Pacifics. No 2 *Northern Chief* looks every bit a thoroughbred and belies the fact that she is now 60 years old as she stands on Hythe turntable. September 1977.
(David C Rodgers)
Pentax SP500   55mm Takumar
Kodachrome II   1/60, f5.6

Right: Appearances can be deceptive, for this view on the Romney, Hythe and Dymchurch Railway, affectionately known as the 'World's Smallest Public Railway' and without doubt the most elaborate miniature railway in the world, belies the fact that the gauge is only 15 in. During the course of a footplate ride on *Doctor Syn*, the author captured No 11 *Black Prince*, the latest addition to the line's steam fleet, on the double-track section at Dymchurch. Acquired in 1976, No 11 was one of a trio of Krupp Pacifics built in 1937 for use at a trade fair in Dusseldorf and interestingly now sports the name carried prior to 1948 by *Doctor Syn*. September 1977. *(David C Rodgers)*
Pentax SP500   55mm Takumar
Kodachrome II   1/125, f3.2

Left: Opened in 1876 as a 3 ft 0 in gauge line to carry haematite ore from Boot, at the head of Eskdale, to the Furness Railway at Ravenglass, the R&ER was re-gauged to 15 in during World War I. The railway's only six-coupled design, *Northern Rock*, heads a westbound train past the restored watermill at Muncaster on a section once laid with dual-gauge track to allow standard gauge wagons to reach Murthwaite. 18 September 1981. *(David C Rodgers)*
Pentax SP500   55mm Takumar
Kodachrome 25   1/250, f4

Below: Amongst the visiting locos to celebrate the centenary of the R&ER was Fairbourne Railway 2-4-2 *Siân* (since rebuilt and named *Sydney*), seen piloting the R&ER's own 2-6-2 *Northern Rock*, built in Ravenglass workshops in 1976, away from Eskdale Green on the last lap to Dalegarth. 26 September 1976. *(David C Rodgers)*
Pentax SP500   55mm Takumar
Kodachrome II   1/250, f4

Above: Three-quarters of the Rodgers family are taking a ride on what would otherwise be an empty stock working to test Kerr Stuart 0-4-2T *Bonnie Dundee* on the 15 in gauge Ravenglass and Eskdale Railway. Built in 1901 for use at Dundee gasworks, it has been re-gauged from its original 2 ft 0 in and rebuilt for use on lighter trains incorporating parts from Heywood's *Ella* of 1881. It is seen here at Gilbert's cutting, between Fisherground loop and Beckfoot. March 1982. *(David C Rodgers)*
Pentax MX   50mm Takumar
Kodachrome 25   1/250, f3.5

29

Opposite: When Adams Class 02 0-4-4T No W24 *Calbourne* was repainted in unlined black livery on the Isle of Wight Steam Railway, it was a pleasant reminder of the last days of steam operation on the Ryde-Shanklin line prior to its temporary closure in December 1966. Haven Street, where *Calbourne* is pictured with a train of pre-grouping non-corridor coaches, is now the terminus of the 1¾-mile line to Wootton, but was once a passing place on the Cowes-Newport-Ryde line. Originally LSWR No 209 and built in 1891, *Calbourne* was fitted with an enlarged bunker and Westinghouse brake before being transferred to the island in 1925, and is now the sole survivor of this once-numerous class. 25 September 1983. *(D T Cobbe)*
Pentax MX
50mm Takumar
Kodachrome 64   1/250, f5.6

Left: A delightful study full of Edwardian atmosphere at Sheffield Park station, Bluebell Railway. Former LB&SCR Stroudley Class B1 0-4-2 No 214 *Gladstone* on loan from the NRM, York, is posed during its centenary year with a train of vintage SE&CR coaches. *Gladstone* was withdrawn in 1927 and, thanks to the initiative of the Stephenson Locomotive Society, became the first engine to be privately preserved. Of particular note is the gabled station building with decorative tile-hanging. 27 March 1982.
(A G Orchard)
Bronica S2A
Agfachrome 50S   1/125, f7

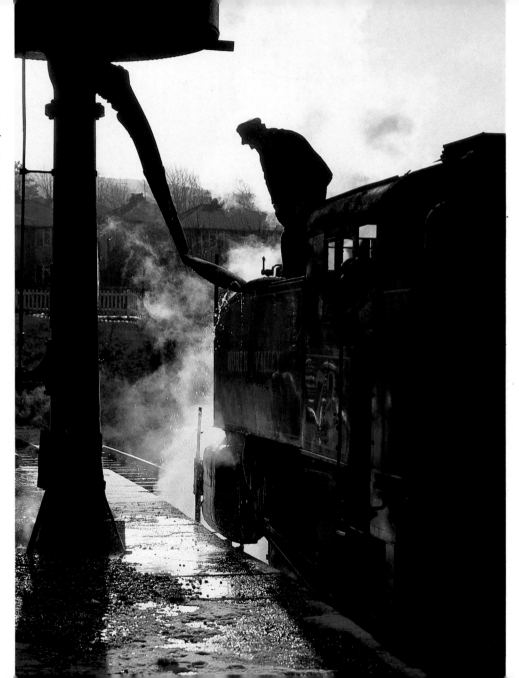

Left: Star of the film 'The Titfield Thunderbolt', former Liverpool and Manchester Railway No 57 *Lion*, built in 1838, was restored to working order to lead the 'Rocket 150' cavalcade in 1980 commemorating the opening of the line. *Lion* subsequently went 'on tour' and for a short period was displayed on the KWVR, the author having an enjoyable journey behind her in an open coach in the rain! In more suitable weather *Lion* is seen 'on test' entering Oxenhope station hauling two replica L&MR coaches. 27 August 1981.
(David C Rodgers)
Pentax K1000   85mm Takumar
Kodachrome 25   1/250, f3.5

Right: The fireman of KWVR 0-6-0T No 72 stands on the tank top watching the slowly rising water level and hopefully will withdraw the leather 'bag' before drenching his feet! Note the brazier at the base of the column. 30 November 1980. *(David C Rodgers)*
Pentax MX   135mm Takumar
Kodachrome 25   1/125, f4.5

Right: Hunslet Austerity 0-6-0ST No 48, one of three on the Strathspey Railway in Scotland, is caught shunting Barclay 0-4-0ST No 3 *Clyde* at Boat of Garten. After 14 years of closure, services recommenced in 1979 on the 5-mile Aviemore-Boat of Garten line, which runs along the valley of the River Spey and was once part of the original HR main line via Dava and Forres to Inverness. September 1976. *(A J Lambert)*
Hasselblad 500CM
80mm lens
Ektachrome 64   1/250, f5.6

Opposite: On a crisp Spring morning, ex-British Leyland 0-6-0ST No 2996 *Victor,* built by Bagnall in 1951, steams through Crowcombe on the West Somerset Railway with the lightly-loaded 1015 Minehead-Bishops Lydeard. Having worked the re-opening train in March 1976 from Minehead to Blue Anchor, *Victor* performed the same task later the same year when the line was extended to Williton. Originally a broad-gauge branch from Norton Fitzwarren, it was converted to standard gauge in 1882 and later absorbed by the GWR. Today the 19¾ miles through the Quantock Hills form the longest privately operated line in the UK. 15 March 1981. *(G T Heavyside)*
Pentax Spotmatic
55mm Takumar
Kodachrome 64
1/250, f4.5

Attractive Swedish State Railways (SJ) oil-fired 2-6-4T No 1928 stands on the turntable at Wansford, now the operating base of the Nene Valley Railway. The adoption by the NVR of Berne loading gauge allows the use of Continental rolling stock otherwise too large to operate within the restricted British loading gauge. Built by Nydquist and Holm in 1953 as a member of the last class of steam locos to be built for SJ, she is seen here temporarily renumbered 74.750 for use during filming of the James Bond film 'Octopussy'. 3 October 1982. (M Squire)
Pentax K1000   50mm Takumar
Kodachrome 25   1/250, f3.5

A far cry from working Copenhagen suburban services for ex-Danish State Railways Class S three-cylinder 2-6-4T No 740 is its work on the Nene Valley Railway. Temporarily renumbered 62.015 for filming, it is seen hauling a train of Danish maroon-liveried postwar saloons and Wagons-Lits dining car No 2975 along the ex-LNWR Peterborough East-Northampton line at Castor, en route for Orton Mere, at the time the limit of working, although 1986 was expected to see the eastern terminus extended into Peterborough. 3 October 1982. *(B Sharpe)*
Pentax K1000   85mm Takumar
Kodachrome 25   1/250, f3.5

Left: The Nene Valley Railway, running for 6¼ miles largely through the Nene Park from Orton Mere through Wansford to Yarwell Mill, presents a truly international flavour. Not to be outdone by locomotives of Swedish, Danish, French and German origin, BR Standard Class 7 4-6-2 No 70000 *Britannia* makes a brave showing for the home country on a 'Santa Special' at Castor hauling a rake of Continental stock. Built in 1951, the first of 999 standard locomotives, *Britannia* was ear-marked by BR for preservation but No 70013 was selected instead. Following lengthy restoration at Bridgnorth No 70000 arrived on the NVR in 1980. 12 December 1981.
(B Sharpe)
Pentax K1000   85mm Takumar
Kodachrome 25   1/250, f2.8

Above: Snow still lies on the carriage roofs as KWVR's 0-6-0PT No L89 nears the end of its journey to Oxenhope with the 1345 from Haworth. Built at Swindon in 1929 as No 5775 and one of 863 standard shunting and general purpose pannier tanks, it was sold by BR to London Transport in 1963 where, in common with several of its sisters, it was engaged on engineers' trains. It still carries the attractive lined maroon livery of this previous owner. 30 December 1979. *(David C Rodgers)*
Pentax K1000   85mm Takumar
Kodachrome II   1/250, f2.5   39

There was a steady decline in traffic on the Isle of Man Railway from the mid 1950s until closure in 1965. Fortunately a group headed by the Marquis of Ailsa leased the railway in 1967 but operating services on all lines proved too ambitious, leading to the closure of the Peel and Ramsey lines at the end of 1968; the Port Erin line continued to operate until the end of 1971, when the lease was surrendered. The railway was effectively 'nationalised' when purchased by the Manx Government at the end of 1977. Due to a failure the previous day, two locos were in steam on this occasion in Douglas station, once the largest narrow gauge station in the British Isles, and sadly by now shorn of its decorative canopies. On the left is No 4 *Loch* while the then green-liveried No 11 *Maitland* marshalls stock for the 1010 departure. Unfortunately the superb finialled lower quadrant signals are no more, having been replaced by colour lights! 23 September 1980. *(David C Rodgers)*

Pentax SP500   135mm Takumar
Kodachrome 25   1/125, f4

In 1983 Beyer Peacock 2-4-0T No 11 *Maitland* was repainted in Indian red livery. However, it was still apple green in 1980 when seen casting a smoke screen over Douglas as it forged up the 1 in 70 gradient of Nunnery bank with the 1010 to Port Erin conveying three additional bogie saloon coaches for a Manx Line party. Beyond the train can be seen Snaefell, at 2034 ft the highest mountain on this tranquil island. 23 September 1980. *(David C Rodgers)*
Pentax SP500   55mm Takumar
Kodachrome 25   1/250, f3.5

Her crew having attended to the single-line staff instrument, Ffestiniog Railway 2-4-0STT *Blanche* accelerates away from Minffordd and prepares to attack Gwyndy bank with an up train. This station, closed in September 1939 and reopened in May 1956, has always seen an interchange of passengers with the Cambrian Coast line which passes beneath the FR at the rear of the train, and is also the station for visitors to Portmeirion, the Italian-style village created by Sir Clough Williams-Ellis. At a lower level is the FR yard, where sidings were laid to facilitate the trans-shipment of traffic with the standard gauge, although this facility has now ceased following the closure of the BR connection in 1972. Note the right-hand running through the loop in contrast to normal British practice. April 1981.
(David C Rodgers)
Pentax K1000   50mm Takumar
Kodachrome 25   1/125, ƒ5.6

42

For ten years Dduallt remained the eastern terminus of the Ffestiniog Railway, but in 1978 the line was extended on a completely new alignment to Tanygrisiau. In order to gain height the new line crosses over the original by means of a spiral and takes a new course parallel to the former route. 1879-built Fairlie *Merddin Emrys* is seen with an up train on Rhoslyn Bridge, crossing the line by which it has arrived at Dduallt, on the 1 in 80 grade at the start of the 'deviation'. With the valley floor here being some 500 feet below the train, spectacular views abound of the Snowdon mountains towards Trawsfynydd. April 1981. (*David C Rodgers*)
Pentax SP500 55mm Takumar
Kodachrome 25 1/250, f3.5

43

Right: British Rail's only narrow gauge line and, since August 1968, its only line operated solely by steam traction, is the 1 ft 11½ in gauge Vale of Rheidol railway, running 11¾ miles from the Cardigan Bay resort of Aberystwyth up the Rheidol Valley to Devil's Bridge, a climb of 680 ft. GWR 2-6-2T No 7 *Owain Glyndŵr*, still a coal burner, storms up to Aberffrwd, a water stop and one-time passing loop. In keeping with its new corporate identity BR repainted its narrow gauge stock in unlined blue livery in 1967, but this somewhat unpopular decision has now been reversed. 22 June 1977. *(Andrew Bell)*
Pentax S1a   85mm Takumar
Kodachrome 25   1/250, f3.8

Opposite: A consequence of BR's improved marketing of the Vale of Rheidol railway was the repainting of the stock in liveries other than BR blue. Built at Swindon in 1923 to augment the line's earlier Davies and Metcalfe tanks, 2-6-2T No 7 *Owain Glyndŵr* was repainted in 1983 courtesy of Shell Oil (UK) Ltd in the splendid lined BR green livery which it had carried until 1967. Sporting a repositioned brass cabside numberplate and crest, No 7, now oil-fired, is seen with a rake of six chocolate and cream coaches on the approach to Nantyronen with the 1030 Aberystwyth-Devil's Bridge. 7 May 1984. *(R Dickinson)*
Olympus OM1   50mm Zuiko
Kodachrome 64   1/250, f5.6

Overleaf: The late afternoon sun dramatises the scene at Clogwyn, the highest of the three passing loops on the 3100 ft ascent from Llanberis to Snowdon summit. Built to 2 ft 7½ in (80 cm) gauge, the 4¾-mile line was struck by disaster on the opening day in 1896 when a descending train jumped the rails and fell into a ravine. The maximum grade of 1 in 5½ is too steep for adhesion alone. Consequently the eight locos supplied by Swiss Locomotive and Machine Works, Winterthur (No 1 *Ladas* was subsequently wrecked) operate on the Abt system whereby pinions engage on two toothed racks in the centre of the track. An interesting fact is that, for safety, the locomotive and coach are always left uncoupled on this, the only rack line in the British Isles. 30 May 1984. *(F Cronin)*
Nikon FT3   Vivitar 205mm
Kodachrome 64   1/250, f5.6

Hunslet 0-4-0ST *Maid Marian* is seen leaving Bala (Llyn Tegid) bound for Llanuwchllyn on the 4½-mile 1 ft 11½ in gauge Bala Lake Railway. Opened throughout in 1976, it occupies the trackbed of the former standard gauge Ruabon-Morfa Mawddach line, closed in 1965, running alongside the largest natural lake in Wales. Built in 1903 for Dinorwic Slate Quarries Ltd, *Maid Marian* subsequently saw service at Bressingham and back at Llanberis and is pictured here hauling a short train of bogie 'toastrack' open-sided coaches and an enclosed saloon. July 1976. *(G T Monks)*
Nikkormat FTn   50mm Nikkor
Kodachrome 25   1/250, f3.5

Left: When the Talyllyn Railway Preservation Society took control in 1951 the line was moribund, having been starved of cash and maintenance for years, yet kept alive by the line's owner and benefactor, Sir Henry Haydn Jones. Against all odds the line was rebuilt by volunteers and upgraded to cope with the increasing traffic, one example being the loop at Quarry Siding between Brynglas and Abergynolwyn, opened in 1969. Seen on the through line heading a train from Tywyn to Nant Gwernol is 0-4-0WT No 2 *Dolgoch*, with one of the original bow-sided 4-wheel coaches immediately behind the engine. 31 May 1985. *(David C Rodgers)*
Pentax MX 50mm Takumar
Kodachrome 25 1/250, f3.5

Above: One of the first tasks facing the newly-formed Talyllyn Railway Preservation Society was to obtain additional motive power, and they were very fortunate in obtaining two ex-Corris Railway locos for the princely sum of £25 each from BR! Built by Falcon Engineer-ing works in 1878, 0-4-2ST No 3 *Sir Haydn* has had four owners, the Corris Railway, GWR, BR and Talyllyn, and carried the same number for each. She is seen here threading along the upper reaches of the Afon Fathew Valley approaching Abergynolwyn. Formerly painted green and here temporarily named *Sir Handel*, she now purports to belong to Skarloey's railway immortalised by the Rev W Awdry. 30 May 1985. *(David C Rodgers)*
Pentax K1000 35mm Takumar
Kodachrome 25 1/125, f5.6

49

Left: After leaving Kingswear the Torbay and Dartmouth Railway runs for some two miles alongside the estuary of the River Dart prior to turning inland and crossing the impressive Maypool viaduct. Looking towards Dartmouth Naval College, GWR 2-6-2T No 4588 is seen crossing the viaduct soon to leave behind the views of the River Dart and plunge into the darkness of the 495 yd single bore Greenway Tunnel, en route for Paignton. September 1977. *(David C Rodgers)*
Pentax SP500   135mm Takumar
Kodachrome II   1/250, f3.5

Right: The Torbay and Dartmouth line, as its name implies, offers passengers splendid sea views across Torbay and on a clear day Port-land Bill can be seen. Crossing one of the major civil engineering features of the line, the stone-built Hookhills viaduct, is 'Manor' Class 4-6-0 No 7827 *Lydham Manor* as it nears the end of the long climb to Churston, formerly the junction for the Brixham branch. 6 April 1985. *(M Squire)*
Pentax K1000   50mm Takumar
Kodachrome 25   1/250, f4

Overleaf
Left: The 18-mile North Yorkshire Moors Railway runs through probably some of the finest scenery on any preserved line in the UK. Emerging from the glacial gorge of Newton-dale is a Pickering-Grosmont train hauled by the unique Stephenson link motion Class 5 4-6-0 No 4767. This engine is now named *George Stephenson* in honour of that great engineer, one of whose exploits was the con-struction of this very same Whitby-Pickering railway. 31 October 1976. *(David C Rodgers)*
Pentax SP500   135mm Takumar
Kodachrome II   1/250, f3.2

Right: After 3¼ miles of severe climbing from Grosmont, south-bound trains arrive at Goathland, a pleasant village in the heart of the North Yorkshire Moors. While waiting to cross a delayed northbound service, Stanier Class 5 4-6-0 No 45428 *Eric Treacy* has built up a full head of steam and sets off in fine style on easier gradients to Ellerbeck summit and Pickering. 28 May 1985. *(David C Rodgers)*
Pentax MX   50mm Takumar
Kodachrome 25   1/250, f3.8

The Mid Hants 'Watercress' line aims to recreate the atmosphere of Southern Region steam in the 1950s/early 1960s and, judging by this view of Ropley yard, they have been eminently successful. In the foreground is LSWR T9 4-4-0 No 30120 with distinctive 'stovepipe' chimney and dome-mounted safety valves. Beyond it is Standard Class 4 2-6-0 No 76017, like the T9 once a very familiar sight in Hampshire. 6 April 1985. *(David C Rodgers)*
Pentax K1000   50mm Takumar
Kodachrome 25   1/60, f5.6

In the author's opinion one of the finest sights is that of Drummond T9 4-4-0 No 30120 repainted in authentic BR black livery, proudly sporting a 71B Bournemouth shedplate! On loan from the National Collection, she is seen after crossing the A31 Winchester-Alton road, soon after leaving Alresford with the 1130 to Medstead and Four Marks on the Mid Hants Railway. Built in 1899 for use on fast, light-weight passenger trains, the class of 66 soon gained the name 'Greyhounds' on account of their propensity for speed. In 1927, in common with its sisters, No 120 was rebuilt by R W Urie and fitted with a superheater boiler with extended smokebox which radically altered its appearance. Note the large eight-wheel tender, for neither the LSWR nor the SR ever had water troughs. 22 October 1983. *(D T Cobbe)*
Pentax MX 50mm Takumar
Kodachrome 25 1/250, f3.5

Left: Prior to closure in 1973 the 'Watercress line' was regularly used as a diversionary route, and in steam days the larger SR types, such as No 34016 *Bodmin*, could be seen. Originally one of 110 West Country/Battle of Britain engines designed by Bulleid, it was rebuilt on conventional lines in 1958, since when it ran only a quarter million miles until its premature withdrawal in June 1964, to be sent to Woodham Bros scrapyard in South Wales. In fine form, displaying typical SR disc indicators, it is seen in Alresford cutting with the 1200 train to Medstead and Four Marks. 6 May 1985. *(D T Cobbe)*
Pentax MX 50mm Takumar
Kodachrome 64 1/250, f5.6

Above: The Mid Hants Railway is justifiably proud of the restoration of the first BR Standard Class 4 2-6-0 to be returned to traffic, No 76017. Based on the LMS Ivatt Class 4, this design had wide route availability and a large proportion of the 115 engines saw service on the Southern Region. No 76017 is seen entering Medstead station, reopened in May 1983, with the 1130 from Alresford. The expansionist aims of the railway have been realised, with trains now running through to Alton. 10 June 1984.
(D T Cobbe)
Pentax MX 50mm Takumar
Kodachrome 64 1/250, f5.6

Left: For the author the highlight of the Liverpool Garden Festival was the extensive 15 in gauge railway whose frequent trains gave visitors the opportunity to see the impressive landscaping and planting of this former derelict riverside site. Locomotives from both the RHDR and R&ER assisted with the onerous task; from the former was Davey Paxman 4-8-2 No 6 *Samson* seen here displaying a tasteless headboard! The original promotors of the RHDR anticipated a considerable volume of gravel traffic which, needless to say, failed to materialise, and the 2 large 4-8-2s Nos 6 and 5 *Hercules*, were surplus to requirements until restored to traffic in the passenger boom after World War 2. 29 September 1984. *(David C Rodgers)*
Pentax K1000   50mm Takumar
Kodachrome 64   1/250, f5.6

Top right: The Fairbourne Railway started life in 1890 as a 2 ft 0 in gauge horse tramway and was rebuilt to 15 in gauge during the height of the World War 1 by Narrow Gauge Railways Ltd, a Bassett-Lowke subsidiary. At the end of the 1983 season the railway was purchased by John Ellerton and was expected to be re-gauged to 12¼ in for the 1986 season. During the intervening period certain changes were made in the marketing of the railway, not least of which was the emergence of the freelance GW-style 2-4-2 *Siân*, originally built new for the railway in 1963, in a completely unrecognisable but equally attractive form based on Sandy River, Maine practice. Now No 362 and named *Sydney* she heads a train of Ffestiniog-style end-balcony coaches, temporarily mounted on 15 in gauge bogies, from the owner's closed Réseau Guerlédan in France. 31 May 1985. *(David C Rodgers)*
Pentax MX   50mm Takumar
Kodachrome 25   1/125, f4.5

Right: The 15 in gauge Fairbourne Railway forms an end-on connection with BR's scenic Cambrian Coast line. On a pleasant summer day, Caledonian blue-liveried 4-6-2 *Ernest W. Twining* eases gently away from the impressive 4-road terminus with a packed train of holidaymakers, some of whom no doubt will be alighting at Penrhyn Point and continuing across the Mawddach estuary to Barmouth by ferry. This freelance Pacific has had an interesting history, being built in 1949 by Trevor Guest to Twining's design for use at Dudley Zoo. Displaced at Dudley by dieselisation, it arrived on the FR in 1961 and is seen here in 1983, the last season before new management drastically changed this railway. 19 June 1983. *(G T Heavyside)*
Pentax Spotmatic   55mm Takumar
Kodachrome 64   1/250, f4.5

The very distinctive outline of US Army Transportation Corps 0-6-0T No 72 makes an ideal silhouette crossing the 3-arch Mytholmes viaduct on the KWVR. This section between Oakworth and Haworth was part of a deviation built by the Midland Railway to replace the unsafe timber trestle Vale Viaduct only 25 years after the opening of the line. 19 October 1980. *(David C Rodgers)*

Pentax SP500   85mm Takumar
Kodachrome 25   1/250, f3.2

Left: A 'Santa Special' hauled by LMS Class 8F 2-8-0 No 8431 makes a very spirited start out of Haworth for Oxenhope on the KWVR. The location is the south end of Haworth loop, by which route locos gain access to the yard and loco depot. Tucked away out of sight behind the 8F is USA 0-6-0T No 72. 14 December 1980. *(David C Rodgers)*
Pentax SP500 135mm Takumar
Kodachrome 25 1/250, f2.8

Overleaf

Left: A superb study of the Bluebell Railway's pair of LBSCR Class A1X 0-6-0Ts Nos 72 *Fenchurch* and 55 *Stepney* at Holywell. Built at Brighton works in 1872 and 1875 respectively, they were originally used on London suburban services. *Fenchurch* was sold after only 26 years service to the Newhaven Harbour Company but was once again reunited with her sister when the SR absorbed the Company in 1926. Latterly both had a spell on the Hayling Island branch where weight restrictions precluded the use of larger power. Although dwarfed by the train composed largely of Bulleid vehicles, they are very powerful locos relative to their size. *Fenchurch* is seen in lined black livery while *Stepney* is in Stroudley's yellow. 5 February 1984. *(M E Ranieri)*
Nikkormat FTN 50mm Nikkor
Kodachrome 25 1/250, f3.5

Right: The unmistakable outline of GWR 'Dukedog' 4-4-0 No 3217 is silhouetted on Freshfield bank on the Bluebell Railway. Created in 1938 by mating the 32xx 'Duke' Class boiler with the 34xx 'Bulldog' frames, it later became BR No 9017. On withdrawal in 1960 it arrived on the Bluebell Railway where it was named *Earl of Berkeley*, a name allotted but never carried during its main line career. 5 April 1983. *(J Dagley-Morris)*
Petri FT 55mm lens Kodachrome 64
1/500, f8

Pockets of snow lie by the trackside as 'Hall' class 4-6-0 No 4930 *Hagley Hall* tackles the grade out of Bewdley hauling 'The Severn Valley Limited' restaurant car train on the first leg of the day's running to Kidderminster. Leading the train of ex-GWR stock in chocolate and cream livery is Hawksworth Engineers Saloon W80969. This section of track was reopened to regular traffic in July 1984. 17 March 1985. *(David C Rodgers)* *Pentax MX 50mm Takumar Kodachrome 25 1/250, f3.5*

The 3-mile spur between Bewdley and Kidderminster, known as the 'Bewdley loop' and allowing through running to the West Midlands, was not built until 1878, 16 years after the Severn Valley line proper. Seen climbing past the site of Rifle Range Halt, used for a brief period during the early years of this century, is widely-travelled Stanier Class 8F 2-8-0 No 8233 hauling the last train of the day from Bridgnorth to Kidderminster. Although built in 1940, this loco saw little service on the LMS for it was requisitioned for war duty in Iran and later Egypt, and it was not until 1957, following a spell on the Longmoor Military Railway, and re-numbered as BR No 48773 that it joined its 664 sisters. Shortly the train will plunge into the gloom of the single bore Foley Park tunnel. 1 April 1986.
(Richard Bell)
Nikon FE   200mm Nikkor   Kodachrome 64
1/250, f4

Right: In steam days the heaviest locomotives were permitted on the Paignton-Kingswear line, but the 1 in 60 climbs from Goodrington and Kingswear up to Churston were, and still are, a stiff test for engines and crews. Although built for routes restricted to heavier classes, notably the Cambrian, Collett's 'Manor' Class 4-6-0 No 7827 *Lydham Manor* seems well able to cope with even the heaviest trains. Although painted in GWR livery No 7827 is in fact one of the postwar batch built in 1950 and, after several years in the salt-laden atmosphere of Barry scrapyard, it re-entered service in 1973. 28 April 1985. *(A J Lambert)*
Pentax SP1000   85mm Takumar
Kodachrome 25   1/250, f4

Opposite: Resplendent in early BR lined black livery, 'Manor' Class 4-6-0 No 7819 *Hinton Manor,* hauling an afternoon Bridgnorth-Kidderminster train, passes Severn Lodge between Highley and Arley. Leading a rake of GWR coaches is Collett corridor brake composite coach No 6913. From Bridgnorth the SVR follows the west bank of the River Severn until crossing it on Victoria Bridge shortly after leaving Arley. 20 April 1986.
(David C Rodgers)
Pentax K1000   85mm Takumar
Kodachrome 25   1/250, f3.8

Overleaf

Fowler Class 4F 0-6-0 No 43924, built at Derby in 1920, was one of a class of 772 freight engines constructed between 1911 and 1940. Following withdrawal in 1965 it was sent to Woodham Bros scrapyard from where it was rescued to achieve fame by becoming the first engine out of Barry scrapyard to be steamed. It is seen on the KWVR blasting out of the 150-yard Ingrow Tunnel under the Halifax Road, the construction of which caused such severe damage to the new Wesley Place Methodist Church that it had to be rebuilt on a fresh site. 23 September 1979. *(David C Rodgers)*
Pentax SP500   85mm Takumar
Kodachrome 25   1/250, f3.5

LMS Class 4F 0-6-0 No 4027 arrives at Swanwick Junction with a train from Butterley, composed of a rake of BR Mk 1 non-corridor and open stock. Swanwick Junction, mid-point on the Midland Railway Centre's line between Hammersmith and Ironville, is to become the headquarters of the Centre and many items of stock are stored awaiting the completion of an exhibition building, including LMS Travelling Post Office No M30225M, seen on the right. Occasional freight workings are operated by the Trust conveying traffic from BR to the Butterley Co's works, served from Swanwick Junction. 3 October 1982. *(Hugh Ballantyne)*
Leica M4-2 50mm Summicron
Kodachrome 25 1/500, f2.8

Left: It is ironic that S&DJR 2-8-0 No 13809 should now be based at the Midland Railway Centre, for although designed by Fowler at Derby, the parent company was renowned for its small engine policy, preferring to handle heavy freight trains with double-headed 0-6-0s! Although the first batch of six locos was built at Derby, No 13809 was supplied by R Stephenson & Co in 1925. After 40 years service on the Somerset & Dorset she languished in Barry scrapyard until being restored to main line condition. Currently in BR livery, she is seen leaving the eastern terminus of the line at Ironville for Hammersmith with a train in the earlier LMS livery. 3 October 1982. *(Hugh Ballantyne) Hasselblad 2000FC 80mm Planar Agfa CT18 1/500, f4*

Right: LMS Class 3F 0-6-0T No 16440 pilots Class 4F 0-6-0 No 4027 as they enter the eastern terminus of the Midland Railway Centre's line, Ironville, with a train from Butterley. No fewer than four of the ubiquitous Fowler 'Jinties' are to be found at Butterley. Overhauled at Derby works, No 16440 (BR No 47357) is painted in 1928-style LMS maroon, although none of the class wore any colour other than black. Ind Coope Brewery are sponsoring the restoration of sister loco No 47327. 3 October 1982. *(Richard Bell) Nikon FE 50mm Nikkor Kodachrome 25 1/125, f4.5*

Left: A pair of industrials, Hunslet 0-6-0ST *Cumbria* piloted by Peckett 0-4-0ST *Caliban,* combine forces to lift a train from Haverthwaite up the grade past Backbarrow, affording passengers excellent views of the River Leven. The railway performs a very useful function in connecting with the Lake Windermere streamers which ply between Lakeside, Bowness and Ambleside. June 1977. *(David C Rodgers)*
Pentax SP500
55mm Takumar
Kodachrome II
1/250, f3.8

Right: The Lakeside & Haverthwaite Railway operates 3¼ miles of the former Furness Railway branch from Plumpton Junction on the Carnforth-Barrow line. Passenger traffic ceased in September 1965 but freight continued into 1967. The original intention was to try and re-open the line throughout but road improvements using part of the trackbed forced these plans to be abandoned. One of a pair of Fairburn 2-6-4 tanks, the only survivors of over 600 2-cylinder LMS passenger tanks, can be seen working the line. Sporting a somewhat controversial Caledonian blue livery is No 2085, seen approaching Newby Bridge Halt; like her sister she was built at Brighton and lasted until the end of steam on the Eastern Region. April 1977. *(David C Rodgers)*
Pentax SP500
55mm Takumar
Kodachrome II
1/250, f3.2

Opened in 1899, the 'London Extension' of the Great Central Railway was the last main line to be built in Britain and formed a direct route between the North of England, Nottingham, Leicester and Marylebone. After 1960, when the expresses were withdrawn, the line suffered a progressive decline culminating in complete closure in 1969. Fortunately the five miles between Loughborough and Rothley have since re-opened and seen leaving the former location is Norwegian State Railways 2-6-0 No 377 *King Haakon VII* with a five-coach train which includes a Gresley buffet car. Built in 1919 by Nohab, this engine has now moved to Bressingham while its sister No 376 can be seen on the K&ESR. March 1976. *(Dick Manton)*
Nikkormat Ftn   85mm Nikkor
Kodachrome II   1/250, f3.5

GNR 4-2-2 No 1, the first of Patrick Stirling's famous 8 ft singles built in 1870, was withdrawn in 1907 and eventually found a home in the original York Museum. Although steamed in 1938, few could have envisaged its re-emergence over 40 years later on the rival GCR route. On loan from the National Railway Museum, No 1 is seen climbing the 1 in 176 gradient out of Loughborough in fine style with the 1650 to Rothley. Although it had been hoped to preserve the line intact, sadly the double track had to be reduced to single, with trains operating over the former up line. 8 May 1982. *(David C Rodgers)*
Pentax MX 50mm Takumar
Kodachrome 25 1/250, f2.8

Right: After 1½ miles of climbing at largely 1 in 60, 45xx Class 2-6-2T No 4588 storms out of the 495-yard Greenway Tunnel and emerges into brilliant sunshine. A further mile of climbing and the train will reach the summit of the Torbay and Dartmouth Railway at Churston. September 1977. *(David C Rodgers)*
Pentax SP500   135mm Takumar
Kodachrome 25   1/250, f3.5

Opposite: The peace of the lush Devon countryside is shattered by the bark of GWR 45xx 2-6-2T No 4588 hauling a train of BR Mk 1 coaches up the 1 in 75 grade between Greenway tunnel and Churston en route for Paignton. No 4588 was built in 1927 and following withdrawal in 1962 was sent to Woodham Bros scrapyard at Barry. She is one of the later series, distinguished by sloping water tanks giving 300 gallons increased water capacity. September 1977. *(David C Rodgers)*
Pentax SP500   55mm Takumar
Kodachrome II   1/250, f3.5

Left: A timeless scene on the 2 ft 3 in gauge Talyllyn Railway as the line's first loco 0-4-2ST *Talyllyn,* built by Fletcher Jennings as an 0-4-0ST in 1865, starts away from Brynglas and heads for the hills with a train from Tywyn. Although originally opened to link the slate quarries at Bryn Eglwys with Tywyn, the TR has always been a steam-worked passenger-carrying line. Note the lack of doors, for all vehicles are entered from platforms on the north side, and also the use of side buffers instead of the more usual narrow gauge centre coupler. 13 April 1982.
(M Squire)
Pentax K1000   50mm Takumar
Kodachrome 25   1/250, f3.5

Right: For 110 years Abergynolwyn remained the limit of operation for passenger trains on the Talyllyn Railway. However, from May 1976 passengers were able to savour new vistas when the ¾-mile former mineral extension to Nant Gwernol at the foot of the rope-worked incline to Bryn Eglwys slate quarry was opened. Seen leaving the former terminus with a train for Nant Gwernol is one of the original pair of TR locos, No 2 0-4-0WT *Dolgoch,* built by Fletcher Jennings in Whitehaven in 1866. 31 May 1985. *(David C Rodgers)*
Pentax MX   50mm Takumar
Kodachrome 25   1/250, f3.5

A Tanygrisiau-bound train hauled by Ffestiniog Railway Fairlie 0-4-4-0T *Merddin Emrys* is pictured soon after emerging from the new Moelwyn tunnel (294 yards) and will shortly run alongside Llyn Ystradau. Above the rear coaches of the train is a footpath on the site of an incline in use until the first Moelwyn tunnel was constructed in 1842, which allowed trains of slate to run by gravity down to Porthmadog. Just visible above the site of the old tunnel is Trawsfynydd nuclear power station, some 6 miles distant. April 1981. *(David C Rodgers) Pentax MX 135mm Takumar Kodachrome 25 1/250, f2.8*

Once the Moelwyn tunnel was built in 1842 it enabled loaded trains to run by gravity down a continuous grade from Blaenau Ffestiniog to Porthmadog. However, when attempting to re-establish a link with Blaenau, the Ffestiniog Railway was forced to find a new alignment between Tanygrisiau and Dduallt involving the construction of a short climb against down trains due to the CEGB submerging part of the original line beneath a reservoir for a hydro-electric power station. Seen here climbing the 1 in 78 grade between Tanygrisiau and Ffestiniog power station is 1979-built Fairlie's Patent double-bogie loco *Earl of Merioneth*, constructed at Boston Lodge utilising the power bogies from *Livingston Thompson*. April 1981. *(David C Rodgers)*
Pentax SP500 55mm Takumar
Kodachrome 25 1/250, f3.2

Left: To mark the 1983 Powys Eisteddfod a special service was run on the 2 ft 6 in gauge Welshpool and Llanfair Light Railway between Welshpool and Castle Caereinion. The noon train is seen prior to departure from Welshpool hauled by 0-8-0T No 10, built by Société Franco-Belge in 1944, and which latterly saw service on the Austrian Steirmarkische Landesbahn numbered 699.01. W&LLR passenger services were withdrawn as early as 1931 and as all original stock had been scrapped, new vehicles had to be obtained, which explains the Sierra Leone and Austrian vehicles forming the train. 22 October 1983. *(Hugh Ballantyne) Leica M4-2 50mm Summicron Kodachrome 25 1/250, f3.5*

Right: The Welshpool and Llanfair Railway has earned itself a reputation for its interesting collection of overseas narrow gauge rolling stock. One example is No 12 *Joan*, a 1927-built Kerr Stuart 0-6-2T formerly in service at the Government Sugar Factory, Antigua. Here she is hauling the 1715 Welshpool to Llanfair Caereinion at the start of the severe climb to Golfa, a section reopened in 1981. The train is composed of a modern Sierra Leone bogie coach centred between two Austrian (ex-Zillertalbahn) 4-wheel saloons. 3 June 1984. *(Hugh Ballantyne) Leica M4-2 90mm Summicron Kodachrome 25 1/500, f2.8*

The Middleton Railway's claim for inclusion in this volume is not in question for, re-opening in 1960, it was the first preserved standard gauge railway to run a passenger service. Authorised by Act of Parliament in 1758, it pioneered the use of steam traction in 1812 and was not altered from the 4 ft 1 in gauge to standard until 1881. Peckett 0-4-0ST 2003/1941 propels passengers travelling in air-conditioned stock from Hunslet Moor (Tunstall Road) to Middleton (Park Gates) out of the tunnel accommodating the line beneath the M1 motorway into Leeds. As a run-round loop had by 1986 been installed at Middleton, propelling stock was expected to cease. 27 August 1978. *(M Squire)*
Pentax SP500 55mm Takumar
Kodachrome II 1/250, f4

Pouring forth clouds of black exhaust from its Giesl ejector, 1953-built Bagnall 0-6-0ST No 2 strides away from Shackerstone with a 2-coach train of ex-BR Mk 1 coaches for Market Bosworth. Shackerstone station, once a junction on the LNWR and Midland Railway Joint lines to Moira, Coalville and Nuneaton, closed in 1931 but is now the base of the Market Bosworth Light Railway. Services are soon to be extended south to Shenton connecting the site of the Battle of Bosworth Field (1485) with the museum. 9 July 1978. *(G T Monks)*
Nikkormat FTn   50mm Nikkor
Kodachrome 25   1/250, f3.5

Above: Adams 4-4-2T No 30583 prepares to attack Freshfield bank on the Bluebell Railway. This elegant machine was built by Neilson Reid & Co in 1885 for use on LSWR suburban services. It was re-purchased by the Southern Railway in 1946 after 27 years service on Colonel Stephens' East Kent Railway and used on the Axminster-Lyme Regis branch until displaced by Ivatt Class 2 2-6-2Ts in 1960/1. 11 May 1983.
(David C Rodgers)
Pentax K1000 50mm Takumar Kodachrome 25 1/250, f3.5

Right: A pair of former SE&CR locomotives combine forces to lift a train away from Sheffield Park on the Bluebell Railway. In the lead is Class H 0-4-4T No 263, constructed at the company's Ashford works in 1905 for suburban services. The train engine is Class C 0-6-0 tender engine No 592, interestingly the only Longhedge-built loco now in existence. Both engines spent their entire lives on secondary duties on the Eastern and Central sections of the SR. September 1977. *(David C Rodgers)*
Pentax SP500 135mm Takumar Kodachrome II 1/250, f4

Left: Derived from the LMS Stanier and Fairburn tanks, the 155 BR Standard Class 4MT 2-6-4Ts were widely scattered throughout all regions of BR, although the WR only received them right at the end of steam, and were no strangers to the Whitby-Pickering line. The NYMR's green-liveried No 80135 is captured between Grosmont and Esk Valley at the start of the gruelling climb to Goathland and Ellerbeck summit hauling a train largely composed of BR Gloucester RC&W dmu sets.

To the left of the train is the course of the original horse worked route which featured a 1500-yard rope-worked incline. 7 September 1980. *(David C Rodgers)*
Pentax SP500   85mm Takumar
Kodachrome 25   1/250, f3.8

Above: The Whitby and Pickering Railway opened throughout in 1836 but had the disadvantage of a 1500-yard rope-worked incline

between Beckhole and Goathland. The NER constructed a 4½-mile deviation to replace the incline but trains still face a formidable 1 in 49 gradient on the new alignment. Blasting up the grade near Beckhole hauling a Grosmont-Pickering train is Class J72 0-6-0T No 69023 *Joem* piloting former Stewart & Lloyds, Corby 0-6-0ST No 62. 29 April 1984. *(B Sharpe)*
Pentax K1000   85mm Takumar
Kodachrome 25   1/250, f3.5

Left: Stanier Class 5 4-6-0 No 45428 climbs steadily up the valley from Grosmont past Green End on the North Yorkshire Moors Railway with an evening engineers' train formed of an assortment of flat wagons and two 'Walrus' 40-ton bogie ballast wagons. Withdrawal from Leeds (Holbeck) shed in October 1967 at the end of regular steam working on the Eastern Region, No 45428 was purchased for preservation and subsequently named *Eric Treacy* in honour of the late Bishop of Wakefield. 29 April 1984. *(David C Rodgers)*
Pentax MX   50mm Takumar
Kodachrome 25   1/250, f2.8

Right: Not-too-clean LMS 3F 0-6-0T No 47383 presents a most authentic sight as she hauls a demonstration freight train from Highley to Bewdley on the Severn Valley Railway in Eyemore Cutting, Trimpley, soon after crossing Victoria Bridge. Over 400 Belpaire boiler tank engines based on S W Johnson's earlier MR design and popularly known as 'Jinties', were built under Henry Fowler's direction for the LMS. They became the standard shunting type but were equally at home on local freight and branch passenger duties. The class lasted well into the last days of steam, No 47383 not being withdrawn until 1967, with no fewer than ten examples preserved. 20 April 1986. *(David C Rodgers)*
Pentax K1000   50mm Takumar
Kodachrome 25   1/250, f3.5

Left: Blue-liveried Isle of Man Railway 2-4-0T No 12 *Hutchinson* storms up the 1 in 65/70 gradient through Nunnery Woods soon after leaving Douglas with the 1610 to Port Erin. Built by Beyer Peacock in 1908, both this loco and No 11 *Maitland* have been rebuilt with larger diameter boilers and are fitted with cast chimneys instead of the more elegant original copper-capped pattern. Additionally No 12 received an arched cab roof and now resembles the last loco supplied, No 16 *Mannin*. 26 April 1984. *(M Squire)*
Pentax K1000   50mm Takumar
Kodachrome 25   1/250, f2.8

Right: Opened in 1874, the 15½-mile Douglas-Port Erin line is now the only working section of the 3 ft 0 in gauge Isle of Man network which once extended to 46 route miles. Capturing plenty of the charm of an earlier era, Beyer Peacock 2-4-0T No 4 *Loch* pulls out of Port Soderick, 3 miles from Douglas and the first passing loop, with the 1610 to Port Erin. In recent years this loco has regained its elegant bell-mouth brass dome, although she has lost her original Salter safety valves. 21 September 1983. *(D Gouldthorpe)*
Pentax K1000   50mm Takumar
Kodachrome 25   1/250, f2.8

Over 850 examples of the 57xx Class were built for the GWR between 1929 and 1950; later examples such as No 9681 were not delivered until early BR days and it is pleasing to see it displaying the livery of its nationalised former owner. The 57xx panniers were widely used in the Forest of Dean and it is fitting that No 9681 has, after a long period in Barry scrapyard, returned to the Dean Forest Railway based at Norchard. Traffic ceased on the 3½-mile branch in 1976 but the line has now been purchased to allow restoration of passenger services. No 9681 is seen at Lydney Junction collecting a newly-acquired Cowans Sheldon steam crane. 4 April 1986. *(Geoff Silcock)*
Mamiya 645   80mm Sekor
Ektachrome 200   1/125, f11

The tortuous nature of the climb from Goodrington to Churston on the Torbay and Dartmouth Railway is emphasised by a telephoto lens. Climbing high above the cliffs near Saltern Cove is GWR 2-8-0T No 5239 hauling a train of BR Mk 1 coaches led by a GW pattern push-pull auto-trailer. Built in 1924, No 5239 is one of only three surviving 2-8-0Ts, rescued from Barry scrapyard and re-entering service in 1978. It is now named *Goliath*. 30 August 1983. (*J Dagley-Morris*)
Pentax K1000 200mm lens
Kodachrome 25 1/250, f3.5

Lincolnshire Coast Light Railway's 1903 Peckett 0-6-0ST No 2 *Jurassic* departs from the line's headquarters at North Sea Lane, Humberston, the first occasion in eight years, hauling an ex-Ashover Light Railway bogie coach. This little known 2 ft 0 in gauge line near Cleethorpes, Humberside opened in 1960. 30 July 1983. *(Andrew Bell) Mamiya 645 80mm Sekor Ektachrome Professional 64 1/500, f4*